Listen to Me my Friend

THE LESSONS LEARNED

Gina Cerrato

Trilogy Christian Publishers A Wholly Owned Subsidiary of Trinity Broadcasting Network 2442 Michelle Drive Tustin, CA 92780

For information about special discounts for bulk purchases, please contact Trilogy Christian Publishing.

Manufactured in the United States of America

10 9 8 7 6 5 4 3 2 1

Library of Congress Cataloging-in-Publication Data is available.

ISBN 978-1-64088-383-3 (Paperback)
ISBN 978-1-64088-384-0 (ebook)

Dedication

My dear Jacob is my son, my one and only and a true joy in my life for the past thirty-nine years. I have told the story that when I was young and pregnant, I prayed to God asking for a son. Specifically, I asked for a son with blue eyes and curly hair. Today if you met my son you would quickly notice his big blue eyes and beautiful smile. You would enjoy conversation with him as he is quite a talker. You would see that he loves to laugh, and how his laughter and smile can light up a room. Note the curly hair is cut short because he doesn't like it.

Words cannot express how much I love my son and how proud I am of him. Most parents do take pride in talking about their children but not every parent can tell you that their child inspires them and brings a world of sunshine into their lives. As a little boy, and now as a young man, my dear Jacob is truly a special person that people love to know—I don't now and will never take credit for this. I only thank God every day for hearing my prayer. I realize that God not only gave me a son, he gave me a precious son. Inside of Jacob there is a sweet, kind, and caring heart; and then there is a mighty strength, powerful understanding, and endurance. And while he is not perfect, he is a perfect example of how to continue on through a life of hardships, tragedy, loss, and the typical everyday situations we all deal with in this world.

As a child I learned about God in church but as an adult I believed in God because he gave me a beautiful son. My dear Jacob is the kind of person we should all strive to be, a person of strength and endurance.

Thank you Jacob.

Contents

Introduction

When you grow up a preacher's daughter you usually attend a lot of church services, meet a lot of people there, and oftentimes get a lot of attention that you don't want or appreciate.

Looking back on those years I realize those church services taught me to do two things very well and consistently.

One: Sit quietly and observe.

Two: Ask a lot of questions.

I didn't always ask the questions out loud, but sometimes we silently question the things we see in this world while longing to make sense of it all and once I learned there was good and bad, and dumb and smart I wanted answers. I wanted proof, reason, explanation, logic, and most importantly, truth. I didn't want any part of unknown, imaginary, false, or fake.

To many I suppose the known purpose of church is to save your soul. In my case I'd have to say that those two skills I learned there saved all of me many times, many ways. Nothing I learned there prevented heartache, pain, or suffering, but with questions come answers, and with answers comes understanding. In my mind understanding brings me to conclusions.

Needless to say, I don't have all the answers but I definitely can say I have some understanding and peace of mind. Peace of mind about living, loving, and loss and I'd like to share it with you and I hope it helps anyone who is struggling through confusion and pain because it grieves my heart and spirit to see people hurting.

There's always more wisdom to gain from truthful answers to our questions, and better examples to learn from, but if your mind has been rattled by circumstance or your heart has been devastated by loss maybe it wasn't truthful wisdom you were taught or good examples that you learned from. Maybe the influences in your life and the so called lessons you were taught were inaccurate, or misguided or misinterpreted. Very often a seed of confusion and conflict is planted in the heart and mind of a vulnerable soul when someone uses their position or title in life to misguide, misjudge, mistreat or misunderstand someone else.

I remember the days when parents were expected to consistently show love and discipline their children, the church was cherished as a holy and respected house of God and people welcomed law and order to benefit and protect the citizens in our communities. There's always been conflict and disorder somewhere but I do believe we have never had so many people using their voice, demanding to be heard and expecting us to believe they have all the answers as if they have acquired some high and mighty authority that's worth listening to and learning from.

Thankfully I have learned a few lessons that have taught me how to deal with both the confusing and conflicting content and subject matter in my own heart and mind and now willingly rather than reluctantly I hope to bring to your attention what may be causing so much grief and frustration and misunderstanding. Obviously I am a student of lifelong learning but if a church service has broken your spirit rather than lifted your spirit. If a death has paralyzed you rather than made you stronger. If a tragedy has left you grief stricken rather than forgiving and compassionate. If you can't understand why pain and suffering and mistreatment goes on all around us. If you live with false hope rather than knowing who has deceived you. If you haven't stepped up to become the best example to your children…then I welcome you to read the journaling and poetry that has upheld me throughout my own lack of understanding. Each chapter is a different subject and is directed at the world around me concerning what I've observed, experienced and questioned. It's a heart to heart type of conversation and within each attempt to make sense of it all, there is a determination to recover, remember, practice, and put forth the beliefs that have sustained me. This book is not my entire life story but when the chapters are combined it is a story of believing in a God given strength and endurance. A story of determination to persevere and to cling to, the God given opportunity for each of us to have our spirits lifted and our hearts and minds fulfilled with comfort, love, and understanding throughout the difficult days.

God bless you, for your efforts to endure.

1

No Safe Place

At around the age of thirteen I had the thought to someday be a writer, and with that thought I also had strong feelings about telling the truth. I didn't know what subject I would write about, but I had the desire and determination to one day help people and hopefully lift their spirits with creative writing.

It was a hard lesson to learn but eventually I realized that many times what we have in our heart can be overwhelmed by what is going on in our lives. Our circumstances, our surroundings, our situations, our influences, and our choices can make or break a dream, a hope, a faith.

I won't make a judgment on whether I was misguided or if I misunderstood but after many years of Sunday school classes and many different church services I walked away from attending those services like a lost sheep wondering off into the wilderness. It is sometimes a difficult lesson to learn or even be aware of, but it is worth thinking about, how religion and beliefs have influenced your life. It doesn't matter what religion, tradition, cult, nationality, culture, educator, or authority you have been influenced by, the common accusation that can be involved in all of them is a criticism that the outsiders are wrong, and then as a result, we can or should separate ourselves, walk away, from people who don't believe as we believe.

The environment that I was born into was Protestant and while not all churches portray Christianity in the same way, the message I heard was, *this is us and that is them and don't you dare be like them.* Also, the world around us was wrong and while we were strictly forbidden to participate in that world we were also responsible for convincing the people of that world that they too should transform, change, give up and renounce their humanity and be like us. That doesn't even make sense and I do believe there are quite a few generations suffering the consequences of the mixed messages they heard as a child. For so many people their childhood included sitting through the Sunday school lessons and an introduction to both God and the Bible and then hearing about how to be good or bad and accepting or rejecting behaviors that are right or wrong. We were formally introduced to God and then came an age and time of more choices and actually facing the real world and then the confusion and conflict began. Ironically, the underlying and confusing option we were taught is that we do have permission to reject and separate ourselves from something that we don't agree with or anything that makes us feel bad.

The conflict sets in because as we are becoming adults we have daily decisions to make, moral decisions to make, expectations to accomplish, desires to succeed, misunderstandings about right and wrong and a big future in front of us. The problem isn't that we have entered a world of figuring out who on earth is right or wrong. The problem is that those mixed messaged introduced us to God as a source of strength and power, wisdom and knowledge but then never taught us that there's a huge difference between just being introduced to someone and the reality of actually knowing them and then understanding, accepting, and valuing a relationship with that someone. Some people have been introduced to God but it wasn't God that confused them, it was the people around them who showed them how to cut off relationships rather than appreciate and learn from them. Maybe you were expected to be in church but a louder voice taught you the skill of refusing to open your heart and mind and the skill of assuming there was nothing more to learn, so then naturally, you had the right to walk away from anything, even if you actually had no understanding of it.

If we believe there is one God, the Creator of life who is overseeing the world, then why would we think it's possible or wise to separate our daily lives, our circumstances, our contributions and our participation with God, from the one and only God who gave us life? When it comes to the subject of separation God's priority and concern is that we *do not* separate, disconnect, forget or reject him, especially as we battle our way through the conflicts of this world.

And so as you will see, it is worth thinking about who you have allowed to influence you. It is worth knowing who you are listening to and where your beliefs came from. Especially if you haven't managed the challenges in life very well or if you have no time or concern for anyone else who is struggling. So now this is me talking back to the confusion and conflict I've seen, heard, and felt in the world. This is me and maybe you also, telling the big world that we live in, that we cannot be discouraged or disconnected from the truthful wisdom and lessons we have learned—because it is God's truthful wisdom that we have chosen to learn about, believe in, and hold on to.

The Puzzle Portrait

Once upon a time long ago an artist took a picture of me and turned it into a puzzle portrait. I was handed the puzzle a few pieces at a time and it took a very long time, decades, for me to know how to put the puzzle together or to even recognize that every little piece of that puzzle was an accurate image of me.

When the puzzle portrait was the completed photo, I knew then that I was never as smart or strong as I had thought. The resilience to endure the difficulties did not come from me. It came from God; the Father, Son, and Holy Spirit that I had invited and accepted into my heart and mind as a young girl. If one piece of that puzzle had been lost, the portrait would have laid in ruins.

It is not a perfect portrait but it is one that shows a perfect example of how one pathetic sad soul can actually be saved by desperately clinging to God the Mighty, Holy, all know-ing Father of all people and all puzzle pieces. I would not wish my struggles on anyone, but I also would not trade my portrait for anyone else's.

If you look closely at the portrait you can see the scars and tears reflecting off the sunlight, but also if you look deep into the eyes you will see the heart of the portrait. It is there in the heart that you will see the spirit of joy, humility, gratitude, and compassion that is simply but truly, an eternal extension of the artist's love.

When I was thinking about how to introduce myself and my experiences I realized there are a couple hurdles to get over first. One hurdle is that I would describe myself as a simple, and at times, brutally honest person, living my life through common experiences like the woman in the following poem. While the poem is sad it comes from being sympathetically truthful about how people feel, and there is knowledge in understanding how people feel, and I think we should be considerate of how people feel. Sometimes hearing the truth may be uncomfortable to some people but I think the end result will be that we are all better off acknowledging the truth throughout our lifetimes of circumstance and interactions. Life can be tough and hard, and as a result some of us tend to be straightforward but also passionate, when we believe our words are worth sharing.

No Safe Place

There is no safe place for my heart
No way to escape the fear
No safe place to call home
No trust when losing year after year

The little girl only going to school
With the bad men lurking around
Innocence not knowing the danger
Can be taken away never found

There is no safe place for my heart
No way to avoid the fear

Even in hiding there is pain
No trust when losing year after year

The young girl only seeking love
Belonging and a place to share
Adolescence steals a piece of her soul
With the wrong crowd who didn't care

There is no safe place for my heart
No way to battle the fear
Heartache and blame took hold
No trust when losing year after year

The woman with life securely promised
Doesn't know change knocks at her door
As the spouse chases after adventure
To realize he loves her no more

There is no safe place for my heart
As I struggle to conquer fear
The aging wears out my spirit
No trust when losing year after year

The sister who confides, comforts and laughs
With a beloved brother and friend
Not knowing with a curve and a chase
Such precious life comes to an end

There is no safe place for my heart
When loving becomes a fear
Going to a place of grief with darkness
No trust when losing year after year

The white-haired lady with dignity
Only hoping, praying for peace and rest
Learns she is fragile, forgotten, alone
When they ignore her last request

There is no safe place for my heart
When living means living with fear
No safe place to give my heart a home
No love left when losing year after year.

The second hurdle is that when I say who I am and where I come from there's really no way to leave out the part about my dad being a Christian minister. So, my introduction does say that I am a preacher's daughter in the first sentence.

Here's the thing about the hurdles: For those who hesitate to open this kind of book because of a formed opinion or attitude about people like me who live attached to a permanent type of relationship or connection to the words, *religion* or *church*, then I'd like to say, I'm hoping these lessons I have learned can help you. Help you because there is the possibility that you too could be living with and benefit from, overcoming, a pathetic sad soul. To me a pathetic sad soul lives in someone whose beliefs, opinions, attitudes, or actions are based on misunderstanding facts and truth.

So then, while we know not all preachers' kids grow up experiencing the same exact situations, I do believe that most people don't like being misunderstood and labeled because of their parent's choice of profession and purpose.

As a result, the second hurdle to get over together is the awareness and admission that we all do tend to jump to conclusions from time to time. So if you are thinking you have set opinions of me or church people even before I say a word that's okay, let's just move on. Let's just be real open and honest about who we all really are and what we do and start with my impressionable beginning.

Preachers' kids know that people talk about them. We know that many times people are watching us, or attempting to watch over us, or attempting to impress our fathers' by being nice to us. We know that it's common to expect the worst of us while wishing or praying for the best for us. We know it can be like a waiting game to see if we will follow in our fathers' footsteps or chose a path of wildness.

We also know that when a person tells a story about a preacher's kid there can be an envious little smile on their face. Or when hearing a story, a ticklish sort of giggle can go through the listener's heart, or, maybe they might just show an outraged and ugly face of anger. Either way, we do recognize the sound of our own names as they echo off the church walls and out into communities. And we do realize of course as the chatter goes on, that many storytellers think their discussion of children who are cleverly defiant or keenly successful has some sort of importance in this world or validates their opinions.

Preachers' kids also get to know the feeling of being both loved, and disliked, and admired, and ridiculed all at the same time. Loved for acting or performing as angels and yet disliked for having the ability to disrupt or ruin someone's planned agenda. And then again either way, we do see or hear about it when many of the people around us are just so relieved, so pleased, when it is public knowledge or ongoing news that we did make a mistake or do something worse than them, or their kids, or maybe even someone from a non-religious family.

Likewise, preachers' kids also get to know and understand that these people talking *about us* and *around us* also make mistakes and are not perfect. And because we live with the preacher and his wife we know that they are not perfect. So actually, it seems that we end up with the advantage, or a head start in learning some things early on, because we have *seen* early on, that there is no perfection in anyone's human nature. And maybe, just maybe, age makes no difference and we do have a better idea of what could be true and what could be false all around us.

So then, while most children are obviously vulnerable little souls, and everyone is affected by their surroundings, what does all this talk do, or could it do, to a preacher's kid? For some of us who may be attempting to make sense of it all, it can either make us be very judgmental or rebellious, like a lot of the people around us, or we can just attempt to accept people as they are. And we can do that, strive to accept and acknowledge people as they are, because we've been sitting on an old pew bench observing, interacting, listening, and paying attention to people for so long that the truth and reality concerning the imperfection of all of us in this world, is and has been all along, our world. As a result, some preachers' kids know or eventually come to realize that they have been introduced to or educated about a variety of subjects they did not choose or care to study.

And as we are encouraged to sit and study, we watch the conflicts that spin around and the ones that concern our relatives and sometimes it's not so easy to tolerate and accept all the behaviors. While obviously I can't speak for all preachers' kids I do know of some who have both experienced and shared similar and repeated situations. As if joined together or related as one family fatigued by idealism, some preachers' kids have seen reverence shown to our fathers as if being a preacher entitles a man to be regarded as the most holy man on earth. And then we observe the surprise and shock that people express, along with the reasons for leaving churches, as if just recently learned, the preacher may not be the godliest man. Ironically, we know that our dad is not God. He might be an introduction or connection to God and people may be experiencing lots of joy, peace, and attention by getting involved in his church, but we definitely don't sit down at the dinner table with God. So that whole competent or incompetent holiness evaluation that goes on about our dads, good or bad, doesn't matter to us and we don't want to hear about it. We only want to see our dad as a dad and we only want to be a child. Naturally we might want to defend him but secretly we might not care if he leaves the church. Like all children, we really don't want to deal with adult issues until we are adults.

Unfortunately, another thing that preachers' kids can know is the possible loss of privacy and freedom that can come with any congregational authority to oversee and educate. We know that as children born into a smothering world of moral and spiritual enlightenment, for some of us, our young minds were filled with conflicting messages as if we inherited a responsibility publicly or as if the future and destiny of the world was our responsibility and no one else's. This was often done while overemphasizing, the power of authority, the behavior of mankind, the history of every nation, and the war between good and evil. Our minds were filled with words like guilt, shame, fear, right, wrong, trust, obey, sin, love, forgiveness, patience, and then heaven and hell, success, disappointment, and failure. But then there was no basic training, no example, and no development of skills to deal with those words. Instead, in the name of God, in the name of love, in the name of family, in the name of improvement, progress, and sacrifice, standards were set. Standards and tolerance levels were set and announced and anyone who did not and does not meet expectations is labeled, judged, and guilty of failure.

And yet while these things go on, some people are so surprised daily at the condition of the human spirit and everyday dispositions. Their questions are: Why is life so hard for some people? Why are there such evil spirited people? Why are so many people negative and unresponsive, annoyed and even bitter? Why won't people listen to advice or join in a church, or a good and wholesome way of life?

Attentive preachers' kids have a few answers for that: it is called rebellion, and it is called pathetic sad souls. It is called having no safe place, and it is defined as being tired of hearing a bunch of talk. It is depressing to never hear any encouragement about hope or joy or miracles or kindness. It is aggravating to sit in church hearing the talk about self-serving goals and satisfying each other rather than being there to serve and love God. It is disturbing to be instructed to memorize the rules and regulations and watch them be broken at the same time. It is strange to know God knows everything that is going on while people are behaving as if he doesn't. Because God does know better than anybody—the church has been used to fulfill chosen and selfish lifestyles for years and the lack of consistency to follow the Bible's guidelines and endure with a truthful unconditional love, and concern for people is simply just a calculated formula. A formula and mixture of messages that adds up to and causes, rebellion, confusion, blame and a lot of sad hurting souls and broken spirits. The people who rebel and turn against church are many times the people who have been to church. Preachers' kids are primary witnesses: seeing, hearing, and knowing that a Sunday morning performance and a mindset of judgments are just a self-serving desperate attempt to gain temporary relief. Temporary relief for some people to make themselves look good, and feel better about themselves while hiding their dishonesty, denials, and the fear inside themselves.

As a result, preachers' kids know that while these same people are claiming their religion as a faith that guides them to talk over people and about people, the only thing that's really been accomplished is that many hurting souls and broken spirits don't have any sacred place to go where they will learn about God and be accepted, loved, heard, or helped. How pathetic and sad that so many people feel disliked in churches rather than welcomed. How disheartening to see people give up on God. How discouraging that even while we can be born into an environment of such serious talks, and introduced to life saving beliefs, and the source of true love and joy; still the mixed messages and the lack of true compassion will keep people out of churches and separated from each other. How sad that repeatedly, history has shown us; there can be people inside the church who are no different, and have no desire to be any different, than the world of people outside of the church—and yet today, we all have trouble accepting and remembering, there is no perfection anywhere.

And finally, what do preachers' kids know?

We know our own intentions and we know that there is peace while we sit quietly and observe and seek the wisdom of understanding. We know how to live with gratitude and we know that there can be simple, uncomplicated joy and thankfulness in living. We know that the only difference between us and someone else is; who fights harder, who ends up stronger, who is more sensitive and submissive in responding to the truth about God, and who has found that safe place for their heart.

And ultimately, we know better than to tell people that we are preachers' kids.

But it was time to tell you the truth. Time to tell you that we know that when we die and go knocking on heaven's door no one there is going to accept our excuse that some person on earth prevented us from living the life that God intended for us to live. With or without approvals, we know this world well and we know not only where to put our trust but also why God tells us to keep trusting him.

So then, one last word about church. While we all know that many people say they believe in God but stop going to church because of what goes on there, which is worse? Going to church and pretending to believe and trust God with your life, or not going to church and claiming to believe and trust God with your life? The point is, either way you are really not fooling anyone, loving anyone, helping anyone, or acknowledging or honoring the God that you say you believe in.

So the next time you and your friends are telling stories about some preacher's kid, do go ahead and talk about me and make sure that you and your friends know that I'm the preacher's kid that is asking you: Where is the safe place where people who are hurting can be accepted, loved, heard, and helped, and learn about the goodness and power of God? If they can't find it in church and they can't find it in knowing you then it's time to stop making things worse, and stop professing and claiming to be something that you are not. Nobody wants or needs more deception, false characters, or dishonesty in their life; we are all looking for the truth. Truth be known God wants his church back and wants to love us, hear from us, and help us. God wants people to come back to knowing, loving, worshiping, and sharing him. It is so very important that we stop our own foolish talk and start listening to him. *Listen to me* is what God is saying to us because he loves us and wants to revive our hearts, and minds, and spirits, and wants the lessons we learn to include understanding and knowing him.

Undeniably one of those lessons does show us that we the people are the ones who create the mindsets, the crushed spirits, and the huge challenges that exist to even put up with each other. We do own the responsibility for our actions and our words and the beliefs that we instill in people. If we don't teach each other how to see the truth about God and the consistency of his character others won't really know God and they won't see any part of God's love in us or in the world. When we are building fear and confusion in the minds of one another at any age we are not building, encouraging, or teaching hope, love, or faith in any area of living. As a result, it takes a lot of prayers, strong will, determination, and consistent resistance to fight off and clear up the confusion, and to resist falling into the trap of believing and acting as if there is no true God or no good church.

And again all this results in the mindset of thinking that we have no safe place to live or love, or to even be loved. The more layers of negative rather than positive, the more fear rather than faith, the more judgment rather than acceptance that we build, the less chance a person has to become a better person and the person that God created them to be. Spirits get crushed and hearts get broken when we don't take responsibility for the type of spirit we present to each other. Our spiritual self and the beliefs that exist deep down in our hearts and souls and minds are personal decisions that we live with, even throughout all those years that we neglected them or ignored how they got there.

That spirit, whether good or bad, is what you are sharing, expressing, or giving back to life or bringing to life. Our spiritual self not only lives inside of us but is also helping or hurting, accepting or neglecting the opportunity we all have to carry on with gratitude and as an extension of God's holy spirit of faith, hope, joy, and love—not only in our hearts and minds, but also into the lives of others.

Observation brings about questions, and questions get answered when you go to the right source of wisdom to seek the truth. I am grateful to have grown up going to church because when I looked at the center of attention there, God, the foundation of the church, I found that he is the source of all strength and wisdom and truth.

While the world may be spinning around confused, and even when I am struggling, I have seen and observed that every statement God has made is true and it is my responsibility to cling to the promises, guidance, and answers that God has already spoken to help me through the confusion. We should all consider ourselves fortunate for being introduced to the God who created us and loves us. We should think about the many people who are living in the desperation and despair of not knowing and understanding how to have love, joy, peace, and comfort in their daily lives.

There are people who not only don't have answers or solutions, but also don't even know where to begin to look for answers. We shouldn't be complaining about the lack of loving and caring spirits and the unpleasant attitudes around us, we should acknowledge the positive and negative around us and direct people to the opportunity to learn the truth about God. If you really believe and know that God can be a part of your life and he can make a difference in how much wisdom and strength you have, and I believe and know how much wisdom and strength God has for us, then we can all make a difference and a better life for each other by sharing what we have learned. And you don't have to be a preacher's kid to understand that; you can find that lesson in the Book of Knowledge, the Bible.

So, in conclusion, if a church service has broken your spirit rather than lifted your spirit, it is worth remembering—misunderstanding God and blaming religions, and people, and past experiences isn't going to get anybody a pardon or a welcome mat and open door to heaven.

Talk to God, say your prayers, remembering, every relationship is built on conversation and appreciation. Stay determined and God will make sure you find a place of worship and fellowship that will not only lift your spirits but will also help you become the person that God created you to be!

2

First Death

Growing up I heard a lot about death, hell, and darkness, but I had never experienced the horror of it. Today after witnessing death several times, my description of those experiences would be: horrific, never pleasant, never the way it is shown on screen or in movies, and never will you know the feeling of it unless you witness it.

The thing I find remarkable about death is that so many people refuse to pay attention to it. They don't want to talk about an actual death, they don't want to think about it, and so few plan for it.

A subject so typical but so unknown.

A subject we cowardly ignore.

A subject we refuse to acknowledge until it gets so close to us, or maybe right in front of us.

First Death

So typical
But so unknown
The signs of aging
Suddenly shown

One week
Of a hospital stay
Quickly, urgently
Comes discharge day

Sons, daughters
Set a plan
Assuring themselves
She will understand

Home she goes
Unable to walk
Rearranging the house
No time for talk

Thank God
We have a volunteer
She can but we won't
Have to be here

Grandmother struggles
To do her best
A fight to go on
Her mind doesn't rest

LISTEN TO ME MY FRIEND

A battle rages
Between her heart and soul
Her choices, her freedom
Someone just stole

Grown children
She loves and worries for
The tears flow
When they walk out the door

A burden she knows
To them everyday
Her greatest fear
They will send her away

Now the caregiver
I assure her, hold her hand
I will never leave you
That's the plan

The nights are sleepless
Damp and dark
The family feelings
Have left their mark

Weeks go by
Nurses come, no one will stay
Forecasting they talk
Predicting her last day

No thought
For me as I endure
No thought for her
They can't do more

GINA CERRATO

I will care
Stay to the end
Finally she knows
On me to depend

But I struggle
I tire losing life
My mind is hazed
With confusion and strife

Love and respect
Keep me here
She talks through the night
Expressing her fear

Her journey slows
Peaceful she rests
Then suddenly she yells
Disturbed and distressed

My nerves now fractured
Maybe broken
She's gasping for air
This day no words spoken

Seven A.M.
I question what I see
Did an angel come down?
Take her from me?

I don't know
I hold her, touch her cheek
She exhales her last struggle
Startled my knees go weak

LISTEN TO ME MY FRIEND

Now here alone
I am pacing the floor
Waiting to know
If she left for sure

The first death witnessed
A nightmare in my mind
My previous existence
I can't even find

So overwhelmed
By all these hours and days
Losing so much more than just her
In so many ways

Warning to all
It will come to you
Will you understand?
Will you know what to do?

Thank God for heaven
With no fear of hell
Today my mind at ease
With her story to tell

A life lived
With honor and simple grace
Knowing with years
We all move to that place

Love was there
Just between her and me
And holding her hand
Was where I wanted to be

The cost, the confusion
The price was high to pay
But she knew I was there
As she stepped away

So typical
But so unknown
A love through life and death
Suddenly shown.

Due to the number of illnesses, accidents, natural disasters, murders, suicides, and lifestyles, it is typical these days to suddenly be dealing with death. It is also very typical these days to be dealing with someone who is sick or elderly and in need of a caregiver. I was in this situation about twenty-five years ago when I took care of my grandmother.

She was eighty-four years old and living alone when she got sick and went into the hospital. About a week later she was confined to a hospital bed in the middle of her living room and doctors said she would not live more than six weeks.

When I say that we should all live our lives realizing that we are examples or role models to one another, my grandmother's lifestyle and good heart definitely comes to mind. Words cannot express how thankful I am to have known this woman. A kind wife and mother, sister and grandmother, who worked consistently both at her job, and at caring and sharing.

For weeks I sat with her while she lay in that bed getting weaker and weaker. Every night was long. Every conversation was important. Every hour was sad. She cried and worried and prayed about her family; and she cried because she was afraid she would be put in a nursing home. Relatives would come and go, but no one would spend a night there. Every night seemed to be a reminder that this was a dying situation. The house was old and dark, and there wasn't much sleeping for my grandmother and me. Through the nights I would sit and comfort her, reassure her, and hold her hand while she talked and cried. Through the days she ate less, talked less, and eventually seemed to be leaving as the pain medicine and illness seemed to take over her thoughts.

As crazy as it sounds her death and my reaction were totally unexpected. It was seven o'clock on a sunny summer morning when she left me there in that creepy house alone, and it was in those moments that the sudden horror of death seemed to take over my mind. Looking back on that situation today the word that comes to mind is *powerful*. Maybe you would expect or want to believe that when you've done, or you're doing, everything possible to care for your loved one you can walk away from that lifeless hospital bed with peace of mind—but I don't see that happening much. Traditionally people speak about love and admiration at funerals but those words and moments don't really reveal their tormented grief. Nobody can say that power is always a good thing and obviously everyone at that funeral sits powerless against death.

What I learned as a caregiver to my grandmother was that I was watching her die. What I felt in the last five minutes of her life was the mighty presence of an absolute power. The power of darkness and the ability of that darkness as it attempts to overpower, weaken and steal your mind, spirit, and soul. While it seemed as if a heavenly angel came down through the ceiling, scooping up my grandmother to take her away to a beautiful eternity, it also seemed that the demons of death hurried into that house just as quickly to carry my mind straight to hell. You can try to tell me that the dreadful thoughts I dealt with were caused by lack of sleep and lack of professional and family support but I can tell you, I'm very aware of where I was and the conditions I was dealing with those days. Like many other people walking this earth today I was the left behind living proof that the sight of death can cause a living nightmare in your mind, and unless you have been there and witnessed a death you really have no authority to talk about it. Then too, some people don't want to talk about it or know how to talk about it. For some it is actually hard to find the words to talk and to tell you about the shattering and shocking experience of a life ended. After all, speaking is not usually the reaction involved for someone in shock. Frightened, stunned, and speechless would be the normal symptoms of shock. No words available, incapable of speaking.

Whether we are aware of it or not, death can take us to a place of feeling helpless, overpowered, and unable to comprehend or communicate. And with its powerful darkness it wants to be contagious and cause more dying and loss of life. It wants to haunt you with bad memories keeping you in constant terror of what you saw and witnessed. The misunderstood darkness of death can be an uncomfortable place of confusion, and sometimes dangerous if you face it alone. You know what you saw in witnessing death up close but you don't know what to do with the memory of it. What do you do with this horrible truth, and this confrontation of being introduced to the unstoppable ending of someone's life? Do you know, are you even aware, that people spend years responding to a death? How many people go on pretending they are fine when they really barely exist and certainly aren't living up to their potential? What do people really do with all these lingering and awful thoughts, feelings, and the confusion that has overwhelmed, crushed, or overpowered them?

> The surprise knowledge of the real and irreversible meaning of the word *never*. Never will that person be here again. Never will you hear their voice again. Never will they respond to you again. Never will you feel the comfort of their love or the simple pleasure of them just being there.
> The questioning and the resistance of not wanting to believe what you saw with your own eyes, heard with your own ears, felt in your own heart.
> The chilling reality that an absolutely lifeless body was right in front of you and then you witnessed the true meaning of dead, empty, not moving, no spirit, no communication, not coming back, gone from this world.
> The tension that overwhelms you with a tightness as if your own blood flow and existence has stopped, frozen up, been paralyzed.
> The feeling of weakness, yet struggling not to surrender.
> The feeling that the mighty hand of death has reached into your chest and grabbed your heart. Causing you to feel that your chest is being twisted and tortured as if someone is choking the life out of you, causing you to gasp for air.
> The feeling of suffering in agony with a fear that you can't explain.
> The feeling or maybe knowing that you are alone with thoughts and nightmares that no one would ever believe or understand.

> The feeling of sadness. You couldn't save them. No one saved them. Maybe they didn't even try to save themselves.
> The feeling and thoughts of continued disbelief, and the urgency to numb yourself, to escape, find relief and be free of memories and reminders.
> The feeling that there was some mistake.
> The feeling of being in a helpless and powerless state of mind.
> Feeling the need to fight or find your way back home.
> The feeling that now you are a part of an unknown world and maybe you have seen or even opened the door to hell on earth.
> The feeling that when this man, woman, parent or child died, no matter how it happened, no matter what the situation, a part of you died too. A part of you died because the demons of death came to convince you; there is nothing but death and darkness for you in your future.
> The feeling of terror and panic in knowing that death is too powerful and forceful to be ignored.
> The feeling of anger, resentment, and refusal to accept that this thing called death did actually take a life away from you. And, that death continues and attempts to destroy, crush, and defeat everyone, every mind, every spirit, every life, and every good thing.
> The feeling of regret.
> The feeling that it is your fault.
> The question, what did I do wrong?
> The feeling of being so lost and always losing.

You would think that with all my church days and beliefs about heaven and hell that I would not have been so stunned by the first death I witnessed. But as it turns out I was just another person experiencing loss. Obviously I do believe today that death can be a powerful and dark experience that can drastically affect us. What I learned is that these words, "heaven and hell," are real places. Good and evil does exist; both taking turns entering and exiting our hearts and minds.

There is a lesson to be learned if we are reluctant to deal with death. It is coming and you can't stop it. Each death you witness truly is an opportunity for the demons of darkness to attack your heart, mind, and spirit, and drag you straight to hell. Forever there has been the battle of good and evil and forever there has been the battle of life and death. Better to be alert to what's going on around you and to accept that, chances are, if you don't prepare for battle and you attempt to face it alone, you most likely will be defeated to some extent in the battle.

Today my heart seems to stop every time I see another death and the same horrible tensions run through me. Each death is a reminder that we must continually face and conquer the demons that attempt to harm, challenge and destroy us. The lesson I carry in my heart that I learned from my grandmother's death is that I will acknowledge any power bigger than myself, good or bad, while at the same time I will also always be aware of any challenge that seeks to destroy me. Hell is the opposite of heaven. Death is the opposite of life. I choose life. I choose to believe that the good and loving God who created life can also give me the strength and wisdom not to be horrified by death. I chose to show love and goodness to my grandmother in her last days and I choose to live on the same way. And although the sight of death may challenge me, no death will ever take my God-given ability, awareness, and the power to choose, away from me again.

For all of us it would be better to learn sooner than later and to always remember that each one of us can have the ability and opportunity to face death with courage and understanding. When you are dealing with a loss, the situation of also losing your own mind, sanity, and future is a tragedy and a result and reaction to death that doesn't have to happen. Anything horrific, every nightmare and everything evil, is a form of misery and destruction. You were not created and born into this world and given a life only for it to be destroyed by grief and darkness. We all have the option and ability to call on the God-given power to recover from grief and be restored to living on with love and goodness and strength.

It's all about choices and whether you're going to live on knowing how to deal with death or just settle for being overwhelmed by it. It's a fact of life that every day you make decisions to do something right or wrong. It's a sad fact that every day many people never take the time to acknowledge that they can create their own hell on earth just by ignoring the so typical but so unknown subject of death. Think about it, the thoughts and feelings of darkness, fear, grief, helplessness, confusion, and being powerless all fit into the one ugly category known as a living hell. My prayer for you is that you will realize and will act on the fact that you need to get a grip on starting to learn and understand that the devil and those demons that haunt you are not the owners or rulers of you or this world. They may exist in your head or heart but you can stop allowing them to exist there.

God is more powerful than the devil and the devil will never overpower God. And certainly the devil cannot take any credit for bringing life into this world. The evil-doers and spirits of this world have limited abilities to work with and they want nothing more than to work hard on you and steal every bit of love and life from you. You are powerless every time you attend a funeral because you cannot stop or prevent a physical cause of death but you are not trapped or helpless when it comes to overpowering the shock and fear and devastation that attacks you as you respond to death. If you are following the wrong crowd you have willingly been influenced and persuaded to follow that crowd. When you are under an influence you are simply submitting and surrendering to something or someone. You are not truly yourself and you are allowing something to control your thoughts. Gradually you lose strength and live in a weakened state of mind.

So why do we cowardly ignore our options when it comes to living and dying? Isn't it the evil one who overwhelms you and grieves your spirit with the darkness, the fears, the confusion, the stress, the tension, and the nightmares? God gives you life and he offers you his love, protection, powerful strength, and the peace of understanding. The devil is not a creator of life or of people, nature, or anything good and he just runs around trying to make you weak and destroy you. He is working hard and desperately right now and his mission is to crush you and take you and your loved ones straight to hell with him.

If you believe in God then you must know that there is always the challenge and battle between good and evil. You do not have the power to stop the existence of evil but you do have the choice to accept God's love and concern for you, and ask God to give you His strength, power, and wisdom to face the challenges that try to defeat you.

Think about it, there are only two possible ways to defeat the darkness of death. One would be to be born with the *opportunity* to live on forever in the light of goodness and love for eternity. The second would be to have the *power* to come back to life and living after being pronounced dead. But obviously most of us don't take the time to even be grateful to God, the only true source of life, for our lives, and then too we say we can live with our doubts about the unknown. We assume that we can live on our own, ignore God, and handle anything that this world puts in front of us. Then as a result we live as we please and our human nature is bound and destined to live under any influence, any lie, or any weakness that we can't fight off on our own. Obviously when we choose to live on our own we have made the decision that there is no importance, no value, no need, and no desire to learn any more than we already know.

It's an unpleasant thought to accept the responsibility of living and dying with our own decisions. While we have the privilege of making informed decisions it is much easier and preferable to ignore the unknown subjects of death and destiny, to leave it to chance, or to be amused and willing to accept someone's self-proclaimed and self-promoted imagination and theories. So then, are death and darkness like the domino effect where we all get knocked down and out and settle for some sudden stop and end? Or even worse, does our mindset of fear just get passed on like some contagious illness that keeps people scared of both dying and facing, some unknown destiny alone? Because obviously if it doesn't matter how you live or die and you have no need or desire to understand how to keep your life going or confront choices and make decisions—then you have simply surrendered to your upcoming and unavoidable death like a cowardly or imprisoned solitary soldier in the evil one's battle to crush you. And, you have not only betrayed yourself but you have also become an ungrateful traitor to those who gave their lives in an attempt to save you.

The biggest lie that you may believe is that you can overlook anything or cope however you want to, and that it really doesn't matter or make any difference. But it does matter to those of us who believe that God already knew before we got here that we would be weak and foolish and fragile so he prepared a way to rescue us. It does matter that God gave us life and loves us so much that he sent his son, Jesus, a part of himself, here to teach us exactly how to avoid a life or death of darkness. It matters that Jesus was a real man on this earth who gave his life, was pronounced dead, and yet lived again to prove the point that it is impossible for anything or any part of death to overpower or defeat God and his ability to rescue us from darkness.

Amazingly we believe the history book stories and anything we read online but we don't believe the story of Jesus. We live with an arrogant belief in ourselves, and the lies we tell ourselves and each other rather than accept the fact that one perfect man stood up against the powers of darkness and laid down his life for us to prevent us from dealing with the death that we deserve. We do deserve the consequences that come to us in life or death when we refuse to acknowledge the one who gave us life. Jesus was the one man on earth who never stopped believing or knowing that God, his Father and our Holy Father the creator of all life, holds all the love, power, goodness, and forgiveness that people need to get through life and death.

So then simply said, Jesus had the God-given *power* to defeat death for us and because he did that we have the God-given *opportunity* to believe it and then live on forever in the light of God's goodness and love throughout eternity. God has kept all his promises and has never lost control or changed his rescue plan. The proof is not only in the life and story of Jesus but it is also in the stories of countless people who have chosen to believe in Jesus and have invited and accepted his story and teaching words into their hearts and minds. Their stories are the ones you should listen to and be influenced by because they can tell you how much life, loving, living on, and facing death changes when we believe the story of Jesus and ask God for the peace and joy of being rescued from hell and misery.

Today there is still thankfulness and love in my heart for my grandmother, and I do thank God that I was holding her hand the morning she left us. I learned an invaluable lesson about how vulnerable we can be when we are not listening, paying attention, and relying on God to strengthen, love, protect and carry us through challenges and the worst kinds of loss.

There is also a prayer in my heart for each and every person who struggles and lives under the influence of weakness and loss of life. If a death has paralyzed you, hopefully you will accept and acknowledge that everything lives by the power of God and learn that the strength that comes from choosing to believe in God and call on God today can rescue you, revive you, and lift your spirits from any darkness and loss—throughout today, tomorrow and forever. Then you too will have the peace and joy of knowing that your destiny is to have an everlasting life with God, simply because you decided to believe in, accept and cherish the God-given opportunity to live on!

3

Tattoos and Church Steeples

It was early morning on a sunny day in June when the phone rang. Mom and I were both getting ready for work. I was planning a move and between apartments so I was staying with Mom temporarily.

Mom answered the phone and I heard her answering questions about my brother Nick. It didn't seem strange or odd to me that someone would be calling about Nick or trying to find him because we knew the way he lived and worked.

Eventually Mom said to the person on the phone, "His sister is here, do you want to talk to her?"

The person on the phone identified himself as a state police officer and went on asking me questions about Nick. "When was the last time you saw him? Does he smoke cigarettes? Does he wear work boots?" After answering only a couple questions I interrupted the hurried officer asking, "Why are you asking me these questions about my brother?"

"There has been an accident," he said, "and the individual involved did not have identification. What kind of cigarettes does Nick smoke?"

"And where is this person now?" I asked urgently.

There was a pause, silence, and then his uneasy reply, "He is deceased."

"And you think this person is my brother?"

Of course, there are no words to describe what happens to your heart and mind, body and soul when you get a phone call like that. The hours of that morning, that day, were devastating. The questions, the details, the morgue, telling my son. Being told that people in the neighborhood thought it was thunder they were hearing as the car crashed through signs, hit and broke a pole, flipped, rolled and landed. Hearing that Nick was sober and died instantly; seeing a picture of the car on the front page of the newspaper. In my mind even if I told you every detail about my brother and his life and death, I feel I could never truly put into words the loss and sadness felt that day.

In anger I could tell you about Nick being one of those preachers' kids that people laughed and made jokes and judgments about, as they repeated and magnified every rumor said about him. The preacher's son, the heroin addict, the alcoholic, the time in jail.

In anger I could also tell you all the people who failed him, overlooked him and didn't care. But as I said earlier, not all preachers' kids choose to be judgmental, some choose acceptance and truth. The thing is, Nick was an even better person than that, he also chose forgiveness.

In memory of my brother I'd like to say—because God gave Nick and I the pleasure of being an honest brother and sister I can tell you—Nick is in heaven.

He is in heaven with the same attitude and heart that he carried here on earth. The street-smart attitude that survived thirty-three years knowing right from wrong with a desire to love and be loved and with a compassionate understanding of love and forgiveness that some people never know.

There is a brutal truth in death. You cannot undo what has been done, and you cannot forget what you have loved. The life was lived, the opportunity was there, the choices were made. Your actions and their actions, your words and their words are now called memories or maybe regrets.

The day we got the phone call about Nick my heart broke. My eyes were sore from crying, my stomach started to hurt, my body felt weak. It took months to question and understand, realize and come to a conclusion on how to accept Nick's death while knowing the details of his life and death. The brutal part of losing Nick to me was that we were after all, so much the same, and so connected as a brother and sister. He and I both so much the same: gypsies, Irish, Italian, players, winners, losers, believers, tough, fragile, broken, fixed. Honest with each other. Honest about ourselves. Honest about God. And strong, we were so strong. We were pillars of determined strength to each other. And now he was gone and with him went the reminder that I leaned on and his strength and his determination to forgive, that I didn't have or hold on my own.

For a time, I struggled. I struggled feeling weak and doubting I would ever be so strong again. My grandmother's death had been the first death to challenge me but this death, my younger brother losing his life, was, it seemed, so much worse than that.

Eventually I learned what Nick wanted me to learn from him. Eventually I took a piece of his forgiving spirit and made it my own. Eventually I remembered that we don't all have the same strength and spirit. We don't all have the same gift to give. We all set different examples. We don't all have the same purpose.

Nick's gift to us was to be a perfect example of someone who had every right to blame, every excuse to deny, every reason to be mad at the world, but he never took advantage of that opportunity. Instead he took full responsibility for himself and he knew and understood what his good and loving God wanted and asked of him. Nick's heart and spirit of forgiveness was and is the example he truly tried to leave behind. If he knew I was sharing this story with you that is what he would want me to tell you. Carry a spirit of forgiveness.

Nick would also want you to know that he didn't have any tattoos. He'd smile and tell you that he had no desire to ruin his good looks with ink. The tattoo spoken of in the poem is the one my son wears on his right arm, in memory of Nick Cerrato.

Tattoos and Church Steeples

Missing you, remembering you
He wears the tattoo in memory of
We carry these symbols of meaning
To demonstrate our love

LISTEN TO ME MY FRIEND

We rise early Sunday morning
Saying prayers in our wooden pew
The church steeple stands above
While we seek answers for life without you

Death like an enemy
Causes anger, torment and fear
We find our ways to battle loss
Accepting it yet wishing you were here

Forever the tattoo is there
Never to be erased
Forever we carry your spirit
Never to be replaced

Church steeples seen for miles
Represent the house of what is true
A precious heart and soul left us
As the heavens welcomed you

Breathing a sigh of relief
With our reminders to understand
The tattoos and church steeples
Provide the comfort God had planned.

A discouraging childhood memory that was never forgotten were the several times that several different people said
and repeated, "the devil never stops chasing after a preacher's
kids and he is horribly determined and will stop at nothing
to ruin and destroy that child's life or use that child's life to
ruin someone else."

While I know that many children suffer many things worse than being a preacher's kid and today children have so much more to deal with, I also think many people don't comprehend how it affects any child when their introduction to life includes such an extreme and vast education about the world and the spiritual beings that live here, human or otherwise. Also, while I am aware that a lot of people say stupid things to children, there's a huge difference between a child being bothered by watching an unreal scary movie, and the situation of never letting a child forget that they are going through life marked, branded, or dodging bullets as if there is a shooting target on their forehead or chest.

And so you see, this is where a preacher's kid develops an attitude to approach life ignoring fear. Since the child has learned to believe in all the Bible stories, and in God, then they also believe that death will take them to heaven. As a result, this youngster concludes that God is the mighty one and the devil is a loser who will never catch me. The attitude is no fear of people, no fear of spending eternity in hell, and certainly no fear to take any risk when it comes to deep down in your heart being true to yourself and your own beliefs. It's a life full of risk, isolation, challenges, and the opportunity and ability to overlook the shortcomings of others even while longing for some encouragement, kind words, or love.

Today when I look back on the way Nick and I lived it reminds me of some sort of little cartoon or video game with characters that can experience or survive any situation. The determined little characters get crushed or smashed down and get up, and then get shot down and crushed again and get up, and it repeats over and over again. There is no fear, no ending, no feeling, no victory, no change to those stories. In real life we all have an abrupt ending but I guess the entertainment found in cartoons and video games is a freedom from acknowledging the pain that we all cause or feel, until the entertainment center is turned off.

On the surface Nick and I were determined and strong, but in our private conversations we were sometimes frustrated by the discouragement and deception we heard and saw but felt we couldn't prove. Our voice was not as big as our God, and we could not outdo or undo some congregation or community's perception of us. At times we did seem to be backed into a corner where we were led to believe that the slightest movement would either cause someone distress or would result as an infliction of pain on ourselves. We felt labeled as a preacher's kids and we couldn't free ourselves from that, but we also felt that we had no rights or the proper skills or authority to speak truth against perceived truths. Even while believing we knew the truth, that people use scapegoats to cover someone else's fear or fall, in our hearts and minds it just didn't seem right to speak out against someone's faith or professed knowledge or spiritual journey.

But these days it doesn't matter if you call it a spiritual journey, a religion or your new or traditional way of knowing God—if the words love, forgiveness, encouragement, and obedience are not in your vocabulary and actions, then you and I are not worshipping the same God. I was weak and grieving when my brother died but I am strong again today. Strong enough to say, you know something is not right when children can tell you what the Bible says better than the grownups can or do. And you know something went wrong when those same children grow up clinging to the stories of the Bible and the truth about God, just hoping, praying, and longing to survive or outlast the false witnesses, and manmade translations, and authoritative statements that insist on changing or disregarding the instructions that God gave us. The instructions, as in those well known and repeated commandments God gave us when he said to obey him and to always love, encourage, and forgive each other.

Those Bible stories are there to build strong, loving, obedient character in all of us so that we can fulfill God's will and purpose for us in life. Unfortunately some people fall into the trap of being the devil's advocate and spokesperson by distorting the words of God as if to imply that certain lives are unworthy, cursed victims with no chance of being a child of God. As if to say God has no power or no hope for some individuals. As if to say that God's love, protection, forgiveness, and guidance does not apply to all children and all people. But was it that, or was it also an attempt and a power play for the spokesperson to instill fear in the impressionable ones so that they could keep vulnerable hearts and minds living both discouraged and scared into obeying, listening to, or living under, the wrong authorities?

Either way, Nick knew the truth about himself and even with all his faults he still had a humble and obedient heart toward God. Nick and I didn't sit in the corner and watch the world go by; we were part of it. Sometimes we lost our way but never did we lose our faith. Nick gained a lot of his wisdom and understanding by reading the Bible in the county prison while overcoming his reading disability. I learned from Nick to never forget that you can carry on a spirit of forgiveness when you understand not only how imperfect we all are but also how disobedient we all are in God's eyes.

There is a rugged, tough, quiet spirit that comes over me when Nick is mentioned and I cut short the conversation. I prefer instead to focus on the church steeples and tattoos and the comfort of knowing that he is in a better place. It's not about a lack of forgiveness, it is about the fact that I loved my brother dearly and other people didn't. And now these days, it is not right to expect me to continuously relive the sadness of my brother's life and leaving, and it is also too late for people to be concerned or ask about Nick, or have the pleasure of knowing him. It was a tragedy to me when Nick died but today the tragedy is about the people just like Nick whose childlike voice is never heard above the masters and monsters of discouragement and disobedience.

When we claim to be a part of the family of God it is not okay to talk to your brothers and sisters as if they are some unworthy, discarded, hopeless souls, and as if a future, sanity, and salvation doesn't apply to them. Will we ever realize how much damage has been done by our words and will we ever change our ways and actually strive to obey God the Father and his commandment to love one another? How many lives could literally be saved if, like Nick, we lived with a desire to love and be loved, and lived with an understanding that forgiveness is an act of love and an acknowledgement of how imperfect and disobedient we all are in God's eyes.

Sadly, we all lost a true and loving brother on the day that Nick died; and sadly, you probably never even knew it or thought about it until now. If only we would listen to our Father we would show and know more love and we would understand that carrying a spirit of forgiveness is a deliberate decision to love regardless of discouragement and faults. Nick taught me how to love and forgive and I will never forget his kindhearted loving spirit.

4

Heart Failure

These days health care professionals are quick to tell us how much progress they have made concerning illnesses, quality of life, and length of life. While it is obvious that medications and treatments have prolonged life there are many of us who suffer the consequences of error when it comes to the health care treatment we receive. There is no doubt the medical professionals have made incredible and mind-boggling accomplishments but it can still be sad and disturbing to hear some of the situations that go on in health care facilities.

While we all long to live our lives out to the fullest it only takes one individual, one decision, or one mistake to change our state of mind and our ability. So many of us are aware of the risks we take when we literally put our lives in the hands of medical professionals and we act accordingly. With living wills, health insurance, life insurance, and religious beliefs in order we think we are prepared. Hopeful to be healed by a medical procedure but quickly and quietly informed, there's always that slight chance of failure.

I guess you could say that other than the first and initial mistake the surgeon made in the operating room this story actually began in the emergency room—when the ER doctor told me that I was, "just a wimp"—"a wimp who couldn't handle minor surgery."

The surgery had been done as an outpatient procedure, I was sent home, as the hours passed the pain increased and I returned to the hospital, to the emergency department. When I was called a wimp I attempted to leave and go to another hospital but I was advised not to do so. Eventually the ER doctor did the right thing, a test was ordered, and I watched on the screen as two sliced bile ducts were causing bile to flow into my abdomen and the excruciating pain. The surgeon had mistakenly cut into other parts of me while removing my gallbladder.

To better understand the pain level of this condition, it was later described by a different doctor as, the same as, battery acid being poured on an open wound. To better understand the mistreatment that I endured; when I finally saw my primary care physician and told her of my situation, both her and her assistant stood there and cried. To better understand the prescribed treatment of this condition; pain medication did not stop the pain and it took six days and three tries before the necessary corrective procedure was completed. To better understand recovery of this condition it has been said; "even when the necessary treatments go well, some patients are never the same after this injury."

A few weeks later as I sat in my house twenty pounds lighter, weighing ninety-six pounds, unable to tolerate food or water, with a stent gouged through my liver and plastic stitched in and shooting out of my afflicted side, I was in agony. To me it was as if time was standing still as I realized that these people had moved me, placed me into a category I couldn't get out of. It was a place, a situation they had caused, and I was left with the results of their mistreatment as they had mishandled the treatments, repeatedly, throughout my time in the hospital. I had fought so hard to live through those days only to arrive at home realizing the fight wasn't over. Realizing those people had not only failed to improve my health, they had also severely damaged me.

Just as there had been no urgency or concern for quick and proper treatment there was also only a minimal effort to make it look like they had done the right things to correct the errors. There was also the fact that they sent me home with their ongoing negligence of symptoms and ongoing negligence of no recovery. Yes, they preach health and well-being, but I saw no practice of that.

A Sadness

I hate the darkness
With its empty sound
Cold damp claustrophobic
No peace to be found

Long unending hours
The walls stand tall caving in
As wounds try to heal
Five weeks now all it's been

Awake, alone, beyond aggravated
With the artificial lights

Medicated, bizarre upsetting nightmares
Reason to hate the nights

Fear, worry, wondering
Where I lost faith and trust
As hospital noises still haunt me
Determination is a must

Panicked, distraught, overwhelming shock
Where did this situation come from?
The losses, the pain, the ugliness
And what have I become?

This sadness could breed a sadness
As if the night's darkness takes over life
Causing the sickness to spread and grow
Strangling breath with grief and strife

I see where the darkness takes me
I'll keep fighting for calm to conquer fear
Holding on waiting for the sunshine
Believing I'll see a sunrise through my tears.

Today I still have pain, and physical complications and conditions that I didn't have before the surgery. Recently and after ten years of enduring—pain and limitations, seeing many different doctors, and many trips to (different) emergency rooms; a wonderful doctor diagnosed both the cause of continued pain and the damage done.

I suppose we have all heard it said that it's the hard times that make us stronger, and it's the struggle, the fight, the desire to succeed, and accomplish that builds character. But I've noticed in myself and a lot of other people that we can get so tired of it all. We often hear an uplifting story that helps us feel better for awhile but then we also recognize in ourselves how physical change or mental anguish can affect the entire day.

As we go through hard times if we look around we will always see someone worse off than ourselves and then too, we do see people get second chances. Sometimes there are many different aspects and tendencies that come out or show up when sudden desperation or loss of self changes our life long plans. Often there will be plenty of time to reflect or attempt to analyze the situation, assuming we don't become addicted to the pain medications.

In comparison, just to name a few of the tendencies, there are the, *I saw my life flash before my eyes* moments that change people, even if only temporarily. There are the people who react by self propelling themselves right into sainthood; as if they can justify cheating death and deserving to live longer by performing a few good works. There are the life altering disabilities that get pity, and then there are the people who take advantage of disabilities. And then there are those of us who spent the sleepless nights, still haunted by the hospital noises, who felt the darkness, felt the sadness and thought; while this situation has been a recent and shocking experience for me and I feel like time is standing still, there are people out there, all over this world, who have been going through these sleepless nights and pain and suffering for years, for so many years. And that thought was so sad and overwhelming—if my time here did stop I expected to live on in a beautiful eternity but these other people living in the darkness, how or when would they ever know any relief, any peace, any hope?

I wish everyone could experience the state of mind and the thoughts I was thinking throughout those days and nights as I was dealing with this situation. I wish there was a way to express just how vividly I understood, sympathized, and felt such a deep sorrow and sadness for every person who lives with ongoing pain and suffering. Any pain, any hurt, any misery that causes people to feel or to know deep inside that they are, for whatever reason, literally and desperately fighting for their lives and dealing with mistreatment. Struggling to get out of the category someone has put them in. Aware of the wrong and incapable of undoing it, but deep in their souls desperately hanging on simply because it is in our human nature to have the will or desire to experience life rather than death. Someone severely hurt them, mistreated them, and overwhelmed them and this life of pain and suffering, this is their life, and they are struggling.

In my struggles I never lost my determination but I faced the reality and had no fear or argument with death each time I expected the pain and conditions to kill me. I did not want to leave my son but I was totally aware that my heart could only take so much mistreatment and then it would just simply become overwhelmed and stop. I expected that within moments I would be seeing my loved ones who had passed on to heaven before me. What I didn't expect were days, hours, years of trying to recover and trying to live with the damage done, no accurate diagnosis, and no recovery.

But time never really does stand still and as a result for years now this has been a true experience that vividly shows how awful people treat each other over and over again. A true experience that has given me, like many others before me, the painful ability to observe, endure, and attempt to understand, the stated claims and misrepresentations of our world's version of success and failure.

✝ ✝ ✝ ✝ ✝

Heart Failure

Can't help measuring
At my present age
Where we all are living
At this moment and life stage

Weighing out the differences
All habits bad and good
Hearts of success and failure
Do we, did we, live as we should?

Years of decisions
Unaccomplished goals and plans
Mistreating one another
With underlying wishes and demands

Unfulfilled not being honest
Never realizing our hopes and dreams
The road to happiness
Never easy as it seems

No satisfaction or contentment
It is a human race
Running down one another
To move on to first place

Is it career, house, or money
Makes you feel you have the most
Or your greed to overpower
Causing you to boast

LISTEN TO ME MY FRIEND

In taking time to notice
So many users now I see
While claiming independence
Yet reliance is never free

Believing you move on successful
You keep us living in the past
Because you never did really improve
Temporary achievements didn't last

Up and down and all around
You continue bouncing off the wall
Trapped in a box called failure
Thinking you know it all

Years of repeated arrogance
Filled with selfishness and pride
Controlling always with an agenda
Planning destinations for you to decide

Where's the goodness, grateful appreciation?
Where's the knowing right from wrong?
Who makes a genuine difference?
Who keeps their faith staying strong?

Why do so many things matter?
Why do we want more than we need?
Why can't simple living, sharing and concern
Be the measurement of how to truly succeed?

Why do we speak of love craving attention?
As if we deserve it to fall from the sky
Why would you think you are entitled?
While trusting people known to lie

Why do we expect to see a perfect world?
Thinking of change, abundance and success
The answer is right there within us
Our hearts and minds refusing to confess

The failures linger on here now
Past to present who keeps score
Repeated behavior with cause and effect
Never responsible but still wanting more

It bothers us to pay attention
Eventually we pay with a price too high for words
Sadly these hearts failed to love
Left with their memories now disturbed

Finally knowing ourselves no better than others
And so late in realizing better people we could be
But still with the resistance to swallow pride
Shows a heart of failure with no sorrow plain to see.

Today there are so many people suffering through the pain of so many different types of mistreatment that it is heartbreaking to even hear about the wrongdoing that goes on. It's not up to me to measure a person's success or failure, but it is up to all of us to at least attempt to understand the difference between living as a victim and how to live victorious. Obviously since I've been dealing with this physical condition for years, and I'm a person who wants to make sense of things, there are quite a few thoughts that have occurred to me.

Of course I must stay up front that I am so very grateful to be here. I am aware that an injury did change me and devastate me but I am also thankful to God that I have not missed out on countless joyful moments that have happened even throughout the days of struggling. I still strive to understand, I long to hear the truth, I accept that we all make mistakes and I realize that difficulties and struggles can be a part of life. But then too, while I have continued on sometimes weary but determined to improve my health, I also still have the desire to learn something—something to feel good about, and something to share and appreciate.

So I press on with my thoughts and my attentive observations and it did occur to me that if I had walked into the ER saying I'd been stabbed in the abdomen, and they saw a visible wound, I really think the treatment would have gone differently. It would have been a situation of urgent care, there wouldn't have been any name calling by the ER doctor and for sure I wouldn't have been told, "Our doctors don't make mistakes like that."

It has also occurred to me that throughout all my efforts to recover I've never met a person who said, "Yes I understand, the same exact thing happened to me." But rather I have seen the looks of disbelief on faces, as if I am a dishonest person.

Also when I mentioned earlier that there are different aspects or tendencies that come out as a person reacts to a situation like this, I did not mention anger. While I know some people get angry and ask, "Why me?"—when looking back on my first years of attempted recovery I feel I was just too weak to be angry. Too weak and too afraid, and throughout every day that I endured severe pain my question was not why, it was, "What? What did they do to me?" I was hurt and hurting but also so close to being terrified of the medical world that there was no energy for anger. I was like a little child who gets burnt and never wants to be near a fire again.

I do understand why people get angry but the surgeon did apologize for his mistake and I accepted his apology and it wasn't his fault that so many other things went wrong in the hospital. In an odd way it is strange to understand that throughout my time in the hospital the employees of that organization, that were treating me, knew that I had been mistakenly injured by one of their own. That is not a delusional or paranoid statement; it is a comparison to the fact that I have worked in a health related field, a pharmacy, and I know how people feel, and what takes place when a customer is given the wrong prescription. There can be a life-threatening or disabling outcome and we are all a part of that organization, and we are all hoping for, relying on, and expecting no errors. But once that mistake happens there is no way to know or predict how anyone and everyone involved, is going to respond. There can be many different reactions to a routine gone wrong, just because after all, neither the pharmacy customer or anyone else are expecting a mistake or for a life changing experience to happen.

So then these days, in many circumstances, expectations are an assumption that can be so discouraging, tiresome, frustrating, and wrong at times. When I was sent home from the hospital, and eventually the stent was removed, the doctors said that I was fine and they also released me to go back to work. And most likely if the doctor said you're fine, other people will tend to believe it.

Then the predictable outcome that happens so often is that people don't know or understand what someone else is dealing with and as a result, the expectation is still there and it can be grueling. I think there are a lot of hurting people who could relate to the disheartening frustration and misery that is felt when they are struggling—because many times to other people—it doesn't matter how much pain you're in and it doesn't matter how much fear you're living with. It doesn't matter if you're honest and it doesn't matter if you are too weak to feel anger. It doesn't matter if you are struggling, they don't see a visible wound. They don't see the failure that you've felt or are feeling and they don't see that your expectations, your good intentions, were met with devastation. They don't see the tears and usually people aren't walking around listening for cries for help. Sometimes as long as you are still alive and breathing, that's all it takes for assumptions to be satisfied. And ready or not, sometimes those assumptions are just adding another layer of mistreatment onto someone who is already suffering.

I've told the details of this story to point out that even when I'm struggling, I consider myself to be like one little speck of sand in this great big world where so many people are and have been, struggling and overlooked, so much worse than me. Physically, mentally, emotionally, and spiritually, others have endured worse and the darkness of those sleepless nights brought those people to my attention.

I don't think it is necessary to list or tell more stories of the pain and suffering people are struggling through because if we were all paying better attention we would realize it through the news we hear, the stories online, and in the behavior of people around us. But then too, sometimes it's as if some people believe that their time spent hearing a tragic story and then having a feeling of sympathy for two minutes justifies their limited compassion and concern for others. These responses are nothing new but what could be a sign of true concern would be if we increased our level of compassion for each other and attempted to understand the categories that people fall into.

My wish, my hope and prayer is that more people would recognize the suffering that goes on and have a change of heart. Our natural tendencies and needs in life do cause us to live with expectations but at the same time the self serving expectations, and assumptions, and mistreatment that goes on is out of control.

Basically most of us expect that the medical field is there to take care of us physically, the church is there to lift our spirits and calm our soul, and the relatives are there to nurture and provide for us and result in smooth success for adulthood. And then all along something called love is supposed to continually run through all of it. It's a good thing to have ambition and an optimistic outlook but no level of academic success, financial success, social recognition, material possessions, or selfish satisfaction is more important than the way we treat one another each and every day.

While I may not be considered a success by the world's standards you could never discourage, halt, or hamper my heart and mind from believing in the God given strength that has not only sustained me but has also increased my endurance and understanding. Some people don't know where that strength comes from or why it could even be considered a measurement of succeeding and sadly, that is part of the reason I believe their agony has been worse than mine.

To me the true meaning of success is to have a strong and loving heart and mind, and to have good results come from what is in my heart and through my actions. Because after all, isn't it the heart to heart situations that bring us the only true satisfaction? Many times it only takes small acts of kindness and recognition or heart to heart compassion to encourage someone. And the more I get to know people and the more I get to know God the stronger I feel about telling people to consider changing their selfish definitions of success and satisfaction. We can be persuaded or talk ourselves into believing that succeeding in our plans equals satisfaction. We can believe that attention or our own self serving pride and entitlement equals some kind of love or love of life, but it's obvious that real love and satisfaction is only felt when we can actually see, feel, and know in our own heart that a genuine compassion has been shared with us. Both giving and receiving can satisfy the longings of our heart. The heart is both the gauge that can measure satisfaction and the motivator that determines and expresses our levels of give and take.

It's natural to have expectations, to have ambition, to talk about the things in life that we love and hope for but gaining anything at someone else's expense, or mistreating someone to accomplish a goal, or ignoring the heart to heart compassion that is needed in this world just makes things worse. It's not a good idea to go through life assuming that everyone is born with some built in instinct or ability to self-lessly share some love or compassion or goodness from their heart. There are built in and internal desires of the heart that drive us to follow our own dreams but I believe the outgoing expressions from a good and God loving heart are one of the most satisfying and important things we can learn from, act on, and share. The ability to give more than we take and to care more than we disregard comes from knowing and learning about God's love and how much he loves us in a heart to heart way.

For those of us who have been mistreated, the caution we take is to never assume anyone's level of experience, honesty, intelligence, or a built-in heartfelt compassion. Obviously, there are plenty of people who could tell us that wrongdoing and the skill of pretending to care is not limited to a few professionals. When time stood still and I felt boxed in those four walls it wasn't anger that rose up inside me, it was heartfelt sorrow and sadness as I saw life through the eyes of people who live in misery. I saw life through the eyes of people oppressed and distraught and from experience I knew how they got there and I felt their despair. While we should all take responsibility for our own mistakes I believe the majority of hurting people have been the recipient of the expressed, communicated and full blown actions that come out of selfish and irresponsible hearts.

For me, so far life has been a lot of learning from my own wrongdoing, my own repeated mistakes, and other people's mistakes, and I have no problem saying that out loud. I understand now why the older generation of Christians who loved me wanted me to learn about God as a young child. They knew there would come a day when the doctor was not a good doctor, the business man was not a good business man, the teacher was not a good teacher, the friend was not a good friend, and that we all have trouble trying to be better or good people. They knew that we all get here the same way, born into this world, brought to life by God, and created as a precious and unique and vulnerable little child. A precious and vulnerable little child that wants to know love but who is also going to need to know where to find strength, endurance, and some understanding throughout the difficult days.

That's where we all start and they knew it. We all arrived here the same way with our delicate little hearts, a soul, a spirit, and then our human nature. But today while I understand that we all eventually go off in our own directions, live what we are taught, and respond to what we see and experience, I also refuse to forget where I came from. I refuse to forget that every single person on this earth was once a tiny precious child of life created by God, the Father. So while precious little children do tend to grow into whatever type of person the world wants or teaches or influences them to be, if we would just take the time to look around and think about it we would realize we also get here with the opportunity to make a serious choice. It is the *childlike* behavior that proves to belong to a tender, loving, joyful heart and it's the *childish* behavior that is owned by a heart that miserably refuses and fails to truly care. It's a choice of living childlike or childish and everyone gets to actually make their very own personal decision.

While it is obvious that the cycle of mistreatment keeps spinning around because we get stuck in that learned childish behavior, it is still possible to remove yourself from that way of life if you will be honest with yourself. There are plenty of sincere and genuine people, who dedicate their lives to actually caring about people, but childish behavior does exist and many times it is expressed by people on a mission to claim power and control and have their way.

We talk about growing up or growing old and we have the resume, stories, and possessions that we have collected to prove years of experience and progress but deep down inside it's never enough to satisfy us. Very often we can see that a spoiled child is not a content child, and childish behavior is self-centered child. Both are still fighting and grabbing for some satisfaction and recognition in life, and like all impatient little children they desperately want it on their terms. Childish people don't want to learn any lessons in life; they just want to live on what they know and whoever will cater to them and promote them. They have no interest in learning the gratification of sharing, or the satisfaction of learned discipline. They are not going to be truly thankful or submit to authority or be apologetic or sorry for their behavior. They want love but they offer no action of love and it's doubtful they could explain love. Their mouth and actions express what is in their heart and mind repeatedly, as they perform the childish behavior of ignoring people, stepping on people, hurting people, to have their way.

So you see the end result is childish little minds in aged bodies that go into panic mode or a mindset of urgency or disarray when faced with a setback or interruption in their plans or expectations. It is really always all about them and they have no concern for anyone else or the damage that they have done. And while claiming to live as independent and free as a bird, they never really left the nest of dependency. They depend on using people, disregarding people and mistreating people to chase down a satisfaction and rationalization they will never find. It makes you wonder if that precious little child that is loved and brought to life by God was ever told or taught any truth about successful living and loving, or if they just didn't want to listen when it was spoken to them. Were they too hurt or devastated to hear it due to someone mistreating them so early in life or were they just abandoned and left to be persuaded that they could live life without ever learning any of the lessons?

Striving to succeed has brought about great accomplishments but the childish behavior we use to gain status and feelings of love, recognition, worthiness, and satisfaction is simply an ongoing insecurity rooted in fear. Childish people live with fear and maybe just maybe, the fear is a lifelong childish insecurity that would come from never acknowledging God the creator, and original Father. The good news is that we always have a choice and it really doesn't matter how old we are since we are never too old to learn. I am eternally grateful that the older generation of Christians in my life taught me the most important thing a child could ever learn and believe in: every single person on earth is a precious and unique person brought to life by God. God, the Father, the Creator, and the one and only true God who offers us the most reliable, trustworthy, and loving relationship and guidance we could ever hope for.

It's a choice of living childish or living childlike, and what a joy and comfort and pleasure it is to acknowledge the Holy Father and live on with a respectful childlike behavior. There's still authority and obedience involved; there's still the responsibility and willingness to be a lifelong learner involved, but there's also a love and security that can't be compared to anything else in the universe. Humbly and thankfully acknowledging the God that breathed life into you is the best choice you can make in life. Choosing to believe in God and be a child of God with a childlike submission to His authority and all-knowing wisdom is a relief that I welcome into my life, heart, and mind. I know who I am in this world and I know who to call on when I'm hurting or lacking strength and understanding.

Obviously many times we go through weak and weary times and it is the fragile and vulnerable childlike person who is over ruled and over powered by the childish person. That's the time for the childlike person to remember that God gave them a life worth living and fighting for and call on God, the Father, for help and strength. God doesn't want his children to be victims of this world. He wants to enable us to be the unique and precious individuals he created us to be, his children, living with his love and guidance to overcome the parts of life that hurt and weaken us.

The more I learn about God, the more relieved I am. It's not a way of being irresponsible but it is respecting and being grateful for the privilege of being here and being loved. I don't have to know it all, or know everyone, or belong to the world's version of love, approval, or successful living. God has a purpose and plan for each one of us and selfish, childish behavior is not a part of his plans. He wants every single one of us to love him, as he loves us, as any father would want his children to do. He wants to see the childlike behavior of brothers and sisters getting along, sharing and caring for each other. He wants to hold our hands through the hard times and one day bring us home to his eternity in heaven. He wants our hearts to be filled with the joy and security of knowing he will never leave us. God wants us to calm down and relax in knowing him, his power, his plans, and his promises. He is God, the Father that we should acknowledge and be grateful to, and he wants us to love him and love life and he provides the guidance and strength we need to flourish and thrive in life.

Everyone in the human race can say they have a father, but saying it doesn't prove that we love him or that we have learned anything from him. So obviously saying you are a child of God can be as if you have just stated that you live with your father's last name even if you don't really know him, acknowledge him or have a relationship with him. Carrying his name around doesn't make you a better person, improve your life, or prove that you have any love in your heart or security in your life. Plenty of previous generations have already proven that a fatherless child can tend to repeat the childish pretend game of make-believe love and security. As a result, your experiences in life may be lacking the true love, support, encouragement, and comforts that every heart and mind naturally longs for from a father. At some point you have to make a decision and an effort to actually know your father, and learn about the good and bad from him, or just settle for being a childish repeat of your ancestors.

Next time you see a child, try to remember what it felt like to be that precious and pure-hearted curious little child who was given life by God, the Father. Stop and remember the joyful bliss of being a trusting little child who believed deep down inside that someone was caring, or would be caring for them, with true love. Take a good look at the innocence of the sweet little children around you and remember that time of life before all the complications and pressures of life changed you. Remember the childlike feeling of wanting to express a whole hearted love.

So yes, this world surely does spin and repeat the cycles of mistreatment, but that childlike little voice inside you that wanted to believe in love was not only right, it is also still there. God not only created you, he also gave you the deep down desire to know him, learn from him, and to welcome the special love that can only be found in our Holy Father. Stop now and remember where you came from, and listen to your heart now like a little child. There is no age that can prevent you from reaching out to know God, the Father, there is no misbehavior that he will not forgive, and there is no child that he will not accept. There is no lasting satisfaction, peace or contentment in our hearts until we accept the love of God, and live loving him with all our hearts.

While some people keep setting goals for selfish satisfaction it is the heart to heart conversations that need to happen so that we can help one another and end the mistreatment that is going on all around us. We should all be praying that more people would have a change of heart and recognize the childlike hearts and childish behaviors and the categories that people fall into. Are we living a life of childish behavior with a heart that fails to truly love and care? Or are we living a childlike life that proves to belong to a tender and loving, giving and sharing joyful heart? Everyone has a father and a childish or childlike heart so it's worth asking—which category did you fall into or which type of child did you choose to be? Isn't it about time to at least make an effort to end the childish behavior and mistreatment?

5

Rise Above

Today while so many people have lost jobs and homes, their health, their loved ones, and have broken up families it is difficult to find helpful words that people will listen to, respond to, or believe in. While we all seem to need some words of encouragement, we may also need to be reminded of the sad fact that loss is nothing new. What might be a new or uneasy thought is that maybe for the first time in a long time it is our time to learn the lesson of accepting the truth about ourselves, our thoughts and our beliefs.

While we may call it loss because something we had is now gone, a better description of our situation may be disappointment. Disappointment in realizing the truth that there is no sure thing. Disappointment in facing the fact and learning that, the idea in your mind of happiness is nothing more than a false expectation. Disappointment in accepting the fact that what you had or believed in was nothing more than false hope. A false, imaginary, and learned idea that you could rely on yourself and others to get you where ever you wanted to go, or to have whatever you thought you wanted or deserved.

Today as we struggle to maintain an ordinary life fulfilling our basic needs, we keep hearing, seeing, and being reminded; there is no happy future, there is no good news, no improvement, no consistent goodness around us, things are getting worse, and possibly there is no hope. Today it does seem that everywhere, someone is drowning in their sorrows. For sure what we need to think about and understand is that while we are suffering through the disappointment what we have really lost along the way is the accurate definition, meaning, and reality of, true hope.

Rise Above

If only I could rise above
Stay afloat
As waves of deceit
Thrash upon my boat

The vessel is damaged
Years of storm
Tragic loveless oceans
Strength out of form

The wind has twisted me
From shore to shore
People, places, anger
Sails ripped and tore

My anchor didn't hold me
False hope, not real twine
The weight of my sorrows
Couldn't hold the line

If only I could rise above
Water pouring in
Praying for a rescue
In drowning I acknowledge sin

How big could the storm be?
Tossing me side to side
Recalling life and regrets
How my spirit lived and died

The waters seem to swallow me
Did this I allow?
Without a life preserver
Sinking stem and bow

But yes, I could rise above
If I accept what is true
Off course with wrong directions
Deep, dark waters to pass through

Did I forget there was a savior?
Saving mind, body, and soul
Navigator of the spirit
Lifting me up out of this water hole

Relying on my skills and self
Manipulators of greed got to me
Storms with thunder and lightning
My heart drifting in the sea

If I had sent out the SOS
Years earlier asking for a steady course
My vessel could have sailed smoothly
Moving forward with full force

Remember now to rise above
As life's captains send us out to sea
There is only one true navigator
With God's guidance I sail on free.

If ever in your lifetime you have believed in God, or heard about God as the Creator of this world, then think for a moment what it would be like if you were invited to spend a day side by side with God watching how he works in and throughout the lives of people.

On that day together, you would have the opportunity to look out over this whole world; watching every town, every city, and all the people. Throughout your time with God he would show you what he does, where he is all the time, and what he is seeing every day and always and you too would see and watch every living thing, every person and every possible situation. You would see people live, talk, work, laugh, and cry. You would hear what they say, and you would know what they think, do, forget, and feel.

While spending your day with God, as you listen and pay attention you would see all the struggles, sadness, despair, and desperation that people suffer through. If you stood back looking at the people of the world you would see and hear those who cling and hold onto their belief that God exists and you would see and hear those who curse and run from Him. You would hear the prayers that go up to God and you would be a witness to how He gives comfort, joy, and peace of mind to those who honor him.

At some point during this day with God don't you think you would actually be amazed to realize how God not only watches over it all but also how he intervenes with his love, power, control, and mightiness? Spending a day with God would show you how he steps into a situation with his goodness and good works. You would see for yourself his ability to comfort the broken-hearted people who cry out to him in pain. You would watch him keep his promises to anyone who acknowledged him and trusted him with their life. At the end of your day spent with God don't you think you would be awestruck and inspired by his powerful love and ability, and thanking him for every detail that he has created, taken care of, and protected? Wouldn't you want to thank him, honor him, rely on him, and trust him with your life?

God has always been available and offering to help us, and yet for thousands of years he has patiently spent time watching us repeat our same old ungrateful lifestyles and our know-it-all behavior. He hears us cry about our disappointments, always wanting and demanding more, and yet he patiently keeps trying to teach us lessons of his love, truth, and goodness. We keep refusing to learn the lessons and he continuously watches as people follow other people right into a sea of disappointment. Every generation and every nation keep making up their own stories of false hope, pride, and redefining happiness, while God continues to prove that the true story of life and love, of joy and hope is in his promised words, and in his true and undeniable written history; the Bible.

If my heart breaks and your heart breaks each time we hear of another sadness, or face another struggle, how much more do you think God's heart breaks? Since God loves us and offers us the ability to overcome hardships, isn't it about time we started applying that ability to our lives rather than continuing to believe in our own false hope or imaginary idea of happiness? Wouldn't you rather live knowing and remembering that you are loved and cared for by our God who is constantly in control and so powerful and watching over this whole world? Wouldn't it be wise to believe in something true rather than false?

It sounds awful to say but if you are counting on, or settling for, what this world has to offer you, don't expect to ever stop living with disappointment. The history of humanity proves that you will consistently and repeatedly deal with more loss, and you will not reach your potential joy as you continue to drown in your own self-pity, sorrow, and ongoing frustration. And yet all along you could have found comfort and understanding in God's promises and his ability to teach you how to rely on him, if only you would listen, learn, and read the truth of his written words and acknowledge his past and present actions.

Times of struggle may be your time to learn a lesson, and while it's a lesson that results in comfort, joy, strength, and trust, you don't end up with the better results unless you are willing to learn and be taught. In the same way that God has provided this earth and nature for your daily needs to be met, he has also provided the Bible for you to study and learn so that he can bring hope, love, contentment, endurance, and knowledge to your heart, mind, and soul.

It's your choice whether to rise above or let the waves of deceit and false hope defeat you. True hope originated, and exists because of God's loving desire to be with us always. The definition of true hope is to know and be confident that we do have our mighty and powerful loving God always with us and watching over us. Making excuses, saying we don't understand, or placing blame and holding onto anger and self-pity is really just a refusal to learn and grow. It's very silly if you really think about it—we want to see our gardens and crops grow and we want the animals and trees and nature to live and be beautiful, we watch our children grow and we pressure them to learn and become educated, yet at some point along the way we stop growing, improving, or learning anything ourselves. It's as if our state of mind became one big complaint and lack of gratitude and that is our version of living.

When I look around it looks to me like everything that has life is growing, or at least it all goes through stages or seasons of growth and being renewed. But not people, right? Troubles come and instead of learning from a hard time or seeking to stabilize, endure, or grow through the situation, we start all the hopelessness, bitterness, distorted blame, and storytelling. Then it's time to give up and find some happy pill, mood booster, new relationship, or delusional way to numb the pain and disappointment.

We don't want to face the truth about ourselves or surrender to the fact that maybe we should change or accept a season of growth and nourishment. It is much easier to find some new distraction that will take our attention away from God, rather than admit you really can't live or have life without him. Sadly, you can choose to look away from God, ignore God, allow distractions to keep you too busy for God, or even replace God with things you think are more important, but eventually you will find out that your weakness is someone else's gain. And ironically those people you trust are relying on you to never learn anymore than you already know.

So, whose expectations are going to be fulfilled, yours or theirs? They led you right into believing in the false hope and a temporary relief that they wanted to sell you, or talk you into, and you accepted their offer while ignoring their motives. Yet now you want to fault anyone but yourself for your stunted growth and overwhelming despair. What prevents you from remembering how you even got here, and how did you even manage to make it this far without telling yourself the truth? When exactly did your all-natural human nature decide that life and living didn't include the process of growing seasons and seasons of storms? Do you think maybe, it stopped when your heart and mind shut off the learning switch inside of you and you settled into your own self-proclaimed wisdom? The kind of so-called wisdom that is confident about whose fault it is when things go wrong and doesn't learn from experience, but who obviously does choose to remain stagnant and dense and then will irresponsibly call a hard situation hopeless.

Don't you find it amazing that it can be so refreshing to look at nature, stand at the ocean, or enjoy the sunshine as if the life all around us is a beautiful gift, but then when you look at so many living and breathing people they appear to be the opposite? Opposite as in slowly killing themselves and filling their hearts, minds, and bodies with anything and everything that will only speed up the dying process for them. Maybe they are overwhelmed because they were never taught or guided through life, but the point is, everything lives by the power of God and everyone of us can learn and grow to be the person God intended for us to become.

Maybe you can't rely on the people around you, but you can rise above the circumstances by trusting in the God that put you here. God did not put you on this earth and forget about you. He gave you the gift of life with a purpose and a plan, and the resources you need to understand the high hopes he has for you. People do change and become new when they open their hearts and minds to learning and understanding God, our Creator. If you remember that every living thing lives by the power of God then you know where your source of power, strength, and understanding comes from.

Some people may be creative, well-educated, or have some skillful way of using you, but there's no human behavior that hasn't been done before. The Bible tells you so and tells you how to deal with every situation—happy or sad, devastating or rewarding, struggling or pleasing. It is a great pleasure to realize you can have courage, peace, and hope as you deal with difficult times. It is a relief to know that you can rely on and trust the God that created you. Trusting is the part of hope that never stops believing and when you believe that God is with you even when things aren't making sense that is when you are learning to have faith.

I thank God that I grew up hearing and reading the Bible stories because it taught me how big this world really is, and that I am just one little person that God loves in his huge design of life. I prefer to try understanding life rather than being swallowed up by it and you will never convince me that any living thing was brought into this world to be slaughtered by circumstance. There is always faith, hope, and love to believe in.

If you are living in despair with no hope, my prayer is that you will ask God right now to help you. Ask God to help you and then get up and take action right now because no matter what you've done God will forgive you and love you. God is not some big, demanding, bossy authority in the sky watching you go through hard times and expecting you to make it on your own. He wants you to realize how you got here and why, and then admit your faults and needs and thank him for life so that he can step into your heart and mind and be your true hope and confidence throughout life.

He wants to guide you, teach you, and comfort you through the difficult days, and help you through the storms. He wants you to know that learning the truth about life rather than being overwhelmed by the lies can save a life—and that is what preachers are trying to tell you. The real truth is that life will never be easy for anyone and it is the Bible that tells us so. Don't give up on hope when God has made so many life-saving resources available to help you. Get up and take action. Turn on your computer, TV, phone, or whatever device you have and if you look for it you will find a Christian minister explaining how much God loves you and how he can help you.

If you have been living with false hope rather than knowing who has deceived you don't just sit there with panic, anger, confusion, or pity, expecting to be rescued. Get up, listen, look around, and join the people who are offering you the God-given resources to learn how to hold onto the true hope, faith, and love. Pick up your Bible, or find one online, and read the promises God has made to you. Learn from the experiences of men and women in the Bible about how reliable God has always been for us. Your life is too valuable to be overlooked, and your purpose for being here has not yet been accomplished so don't you dare drown in a storm. Reach out to believing in true hope and the helpline that God has put in place for you. Then storms will pass, the calm and peace will come to you, and then it will be God you can thank for literally saving you!

6

A Grandson's Prayer

I've shared a few thoughts, asked a few questions, and as I said from the beginning I do ask a lot of questions. So, did we get over the hurdles? Are we there yet? You see I just keep asking questions and like a child I want to know where we are going and if we are there yet. I just want to know if we are safe and secure and going in the right direction.

But real life childhood is only temporary, isn't it? Eventually we have to balance out our childlike submission to God, and our youthful spirit, with the privilege of aged experience, and become responsible adults. Sometimes it just doesn't seem that there are enough people around who are actually showing us how to do that or making sure we get there.

A Grandson's Prayer

Dear God I need to talk to you
About these grown-ups around me
They make me cry and be afraid
Cause of the things I hear and see

I love my Daddy so much
His hugs are so safe and strong
He teaches me with his patience
And helps me when I'm wrong

And Mommy can be a silly girl
All girls are weird that way
I love her but don't like it
She doesn't get it how boys play

God you know I'm only eight
No reason for me to think ahead
But all this talk and what I see
Makes me think of dying and the dead

One little thought and tears start
I can't control the way I feel
I tell them it's allergies, I feel sick
But I'm sad and so scared it's real

People are grouchy and ugly
Smoking and drinking and getting old
Arguing, no jobs, no paychecks
Fighting about their houses getting sold

I know I don't want to grow up
It's more scary to me every day
I say it's just the way I am
Only told grandma I feel this way

Moms, Dads, everywhere
Relatives, cousins and a half brother
Her kids, his kids, their friends
Don't get along with each other

Grandma said I could talk to you
Said she talks to you every day
Told me you created this whole world
So she knew I'd be okay

But God this place is scary
Bad people and who is good?
Afraid of what might happen
I'd tell them if I could

But crying I say I'm tired
Daddy holds me and I fall asleep
Then waking up in different houses
Which room is mine to keep?

Every day is always different
I have a feeling something is wrong
They ask me where I want to go
Never knowing where I belong

So God I think my heart broke
And I know I need it to survive

It's a pain like I could be dying
Who can fix it and keep me alive?

Grandma told me you could help
So if you're listening way up there
I'm just a little boy who's hurt
And I need to know you care

I could try to remember
That you grew every flower and tree
So if you're taking care of this whole world
You could probably take care of me

But I still get afraid and worried
About the people I love and adore
So don't let grandma forget to pray
And I'll know you heard us for sure.

When I first introduced myself in chapter one I realized all along that just because I care about people there is no guarantee people will listen, agree or pay attention to what I say. No, people will pay attention to what you do and always, what you do is one true and visible version of the person that you are deep inside versus who you claim to be.

While I did describe myself as someone living a simple and truthful life, I also said that I was determined, so allow me to introduce myself again. Although I am a pathetic sad soul at times whose attitude and actions are sometimes the result of both misunderstanding and human nature, no one has ever changed what is deep inside my heart. What I do with my poetry and what I am attempting to do is share some of the lessons I've learned and the beliefs that have sustained me. Obviously it is sometimes the most painful experience that can teach us the most valuable lesson. I can say that life has sometimes been difficult, but I know in my heart that my life has been no more difficult than anyone else's life. There's a great advantage to growing up in God's house and I'm very thankful God put me there.

I grew up learning about God but I also learned that believing in God is a choice and an action that each of us either acknowledge or ignore. I am truly thankful to be here and also very thankful for every example and act of God's love and goodness that I have ever seen. I chose to believe in God as a child because I wanted him in my heart and life and I continued to believe in God and love God with heartfelt gratitude.

Today I'm telling you that I also believe in God because of the actions and miracles I have seen God do year after year. Countless miracles like when I prayed to God and asked for a son, he heard me and responded by giving me a son, my dear Jacob, a precious son with blue eyes and curly hair. In my mind it only took one answered prayer, one miracle of prayer, for me to acknowledge that everything I was taught about God is true. And while you don't know all the details of my life, I can tell you for sure, God knew exactly what he was doing and why when he saw what was in a young girl's heart and gave her the pleasure of having the son she asked for.

No one can convince me of coincidence or false explanations and that is a belief I am determined to share. My dear Jacob, my son, is living proof that God is with us always and hears us when we speak to him. Our response should be eternal joy and gratitude for the life and love that God gives each of us. And I won't keep asking, but I wonder, Why would it take more than one answered prayer, why would it take more than one miracle before a person would actually begin to acknowledge, share, and act on believing in God? Because I'll tell you the outcome of showing no appreciation for the miracles; if you believe in God and his miracles and you don't act on your belief then don't expect anyone else to start believing in the miracles.

Don't expect more people to believe in miracles if you didn't provide any explanation, or provide any example of the lessons you've learned about God. Faith doesn't just show up. Faith is taught by example and learned. And according to my grandson and many other little broken-hearted children today, this is a scary world without faith, hope, or love. God didn't give us these children to ignore and he doesn't answer prayers only to be forgotten. He keeps proving his love and consistency to us through his actions, but we don't prove anything to anyone if we don't take action to prove him right. And because of this we never stop struggling.

As a result, we can't be the person God created us to be because we allow people to influence us. We can't deal with death because we feel overpowered by the unknown and unfamiliar challenges. We don't carry a spirit of love and forgiveness because we don't acknowledge our own imperfection and God's instructions. We cause and suffer mistreatment because we lack heart to heart compassion and prefer to be selfish and childish. We can't rise above our problems because we aren't willing to learn. We can't teach our children because we won't lead by example.

How wrong and heartbreaking it is to know that the cause of our little children being so sad and afraid is because of our refusal to even try to be better people. And then what is the result when we don't set good examples or try to be a better person? It will be obvious—as a little child watches you ignore God they won't believe in God or become the person God created them to be. They won't know how to deal with your death or anyone else's. They will not be encouraged or obedient, and where will they learn how to forgive, or how to have a heart filled with genuine love? Should they be expected to struggle through life never really knowing what false hope is? Is that really how you want to leave your children? Is that the type of person you want them to grow up to be? There are bad habits, patterns, and learned behaviors all around us, is that the type of influence and example our children should learn and see? What example of love and all things good do we really give and leave to our children? Shouldn't we be striving to prevent our children from making the same mistakes we've made? The repeated mistakes that keep people confused and afraid and fragile and alone.

God's desire is to encourage, and help you and your loved ones—help you to be strong when everyone around you seems weak. Today can be the day you realize now is the time to talk to God, pray to God, and rely on God's love, guidance, and possibility of miracles. If you will rely on the truthful wisdom that God can teach you and learn to trust in God, the result will be that through your actions both you and your loved ones will see, and experience God's gift of love and joy.

My everyday prayer for you is that you will find that safe place for your heart with God and you will accept God into your heart and life and ask him to help you overcome every challenge and fear. My prayer is that you will use your mind to understand that what is in your heart does matter.

I hope you know that God gave us the ultimate example, Jesus, to show us how to live and die and carry on his spirit of love and forgiveness. I hope you know that just as we want to carry on the spirit of our loved ones who have passed on before us, we can also carry the spirit of Jesus who lived and died, and defeated death by living again. I hope you know he did that and went back to heaven to be an example of God's true love, power, and forgiveness. The perfect example, to show us how to carry God's Holy Spirit with us always and to believe for sure that we can live on both now and one day in heaven.

My prayer for you is that you will learn and remember that God keeps his promises and that you can rise up and out of your sorrows and become the person God created you to be. And I hope that you will decide to join the family of God and make an effort to show us how to live on and love more by striving to be an example of how God helps us endure.

In conclusion the question is—what are your hopes and prayers about? If you haven't stepped up to be the best example to your children or a good example to anyone— what are your true hopes? Are you at least praying for the precious little children who need to know they are loved? Are you remembering how it feels to be a child? Are you praying and asking God to keep you strong and determined so you can share and give the children and other people around you the secure foundation of God's true hope, faith, and love to stand on? Are you at least thankful, for anything? If you are, don't tell me; tell God and your children, and your loved ones. Show and tell your loved ones the lessons you have learned because they are the ones who need to hear from you. And then for sure one day we will all be thanking God together—when you, your children, all your loved ones, and all my loved ones are living with grateful hearts in the beauty and love of heaven!

Correction of Thoughts

The Creator not an inventor
A house not a mansion
A purpose not a profession
A Holy Spirit not a saint
A mentor not an idol
A Bible story not a news story
A son not a hero
A daughter not a princess
A mother not a queen
A father not a king
A faith not a risk
A hope not an illusion
A love not a fantasy
A truth not a denial
A god not a myth
An example not a reputation
A freedom not a rule
A service not a slave
A health not a hazard
A mind not an ignorance
A heart not a snob
A welcome not a stare
A patience not a greed
An endurance not an end
A memory not a grief

An honor not a chore
A prayer not a dream
An understanding not a fear
A stability not an insecurity
A forgiveness not a judgment
A smile not a frown.

Take Me with You

Quietly I sat crying in the backyard
As the sun was dropping behind the trees
Reliving the conversations and heartbreak
Saying God help me please

Around the corner of the house
Came a man and sat down next to me
With a strength and beauty in his eyes
I could tell there was only one person this could be

He kindly asked, "How are you?
I saw you crying and knew you had a bad day
I know you've been calling on God our father
So I stopped by to tell you, it will all turn out okay

Living here can be overwhelming and hard
As you know I went though it myself years ago
But my promises are kept to you every moment
And I see your good intentions, with all the love you show."

Then he stood and took my hands in his
As fear shot through me that he was about to leave
"No wait, take me with you!" I blurted out
"They don't understand and won't listen or believe"

"Precious one," he said with a gracious smile
While firming the grip on my hands
"No, you take me with you
Allowing my spirit to stay and comfort
Who is it that misunderstands?"

I bowed my head not wanting to let go
Thinking still of how cold-hearted this world can be
Again, he spoke, slowly backing away
"Take my love and strength with you
And others will learn to rely on me."

Printed in the USA
CPSIA information can be obtained
at www.ICGtesting.com
JSHW010833011123
50973JS00012B/112